T0417584

AuthorHouse™
1663 Liberty Drive
Bloomington, IN 47403
www.authorhouse.com
Phone: 1 (800) 839-8640

© 2017 Horacio Sanchez. All rights reserved.

No part of this book may be reproduced, stored in a retrieval system,
or transmitted by any means without the written permission of the author.

Published by AuthorHouse 07/13/2017

ISBN: 978-1-5246-9954-3 (sc)
ISBN: 978-1-5246-9953-6 (e)

Library of Congress Control Number: 2017910756

Print information available on the last page.

This book is printed on acid-free paper.

Because of the dynamic nature of the Internet, any web addresses or links contained in this book may have changed since publication and may no longer be valid. The views expressed in this work are solely those of the author and do not necessarily reflect the views of the publisher, and the publisher hereby disclaims any responsibility for them.

authorHOUSE®

Architecture FOR KIDS

Horacio Sanchez

I dedicate this book to my family and friends. To my daughter Constanza, my son Andres, and my daughter Almudena who gave me their strength, and energy, necessarily to pursue my dream. I am grateful beyond words for their love, wisdom, smiles, and inspiration. This book is also dedicated to my wife Vera, my mother Cecilia, my brother Patricio, and my sister Fernanda. One cannot complete something like this without the support of family. I would also like to dedicate this book posthumously to my grandfather Pata, who set an example for me and who encouraged me and believed in me when I doubted myself.

Thank You!

To the Future Architects

Architecture is my passion! It is an art, as well as a discipline that helps you transform your creativity and ideas into something real. Architecture will help you to develop a "design thinking" mentality. In other words, you will learn to see things in a different way, with more detail, focused on the design and space of elements.

In this book, I will show you how architects develop ideas from single forms like squares, rectangles, circles, or even triangles geometric forms that you study in school but also that you can identify in places that you visit in your daily life or at home. You will also see how color, textures, and light play with the other elements to create buildings or public spaces like parks, plazas, cities or landscapes.

This book is for you, future architect or designer. If you decide to follow the architecture path, I can guarantee you that it is going to be an amazing journey!

Horacio Sanchez

Architecture for Kids

Table of Contents

R001	History of Architecture	1
R002	First Steps of Design	6
R003	The Forms	13
R004	The Colors	16
R005	The Textures	18
R006	Dimensions and Light Concepts	20
R007	Your First Project	23
	Index	

Photo Credits are located in the Index Page.

History of Architecture

Photo Credit: doomko/Collection: iStock/Thinkstock
468111742

Architecture opened my eyes and my imagination to a world with no limits

History of Architecture

The history of architecture starts with the first human settlements in the Neolithic Age. Architecture evolved as civilizations evolved.

Timeline (top)

- **P2-R001 — Neolithic Age** (10,000 BC – 6th Century BC)
- **P2-R002 — Egypt** — Giza Pyramid: Use of Mud Brick and Stone
- **P2-R003 — Rome** — Coliseum of Rome: Use of Arches and Domes (900BC – 1st Century)
- **P2-R004 — Persian** — Design of Gardens and Pavilions (509BC – 4th Century)
- **P2-R010 — Japan** — Carved Roofs, Use of Screens or Paper Walls (1185 – 1573)

Timeline (bottom)

- **P2-R005 — Mesopotamia** — Development of Urban Planning (Ziggurats). Ziggurats were huge pyramidal temple towers.
- **P2-R006 — Greece** — The Parthenon Columns (Architrave)
- **P2-R007 — Byzantine** — Influenced by the Roman and Greek Architecture
- **P2-R008 — Islamic** — Dome of the Rock: Influenced by Persian, Roman, and Byzantine
- **P2-R009 — China** — Design with Balance: Great Wall and Pagodas (First Centuries)

Mesopotamians contributed to the field of urban planning with the construction of cities divided in areas like residential, mixed-use, commercial, and civic spaces. Streets and roads were also incorporated.

Photo Credits are located in the Index Page.

2

History of Architecture

Do some research on the words or concepts that you do not know or you do not understand. Take notes and start building your architect's journal.

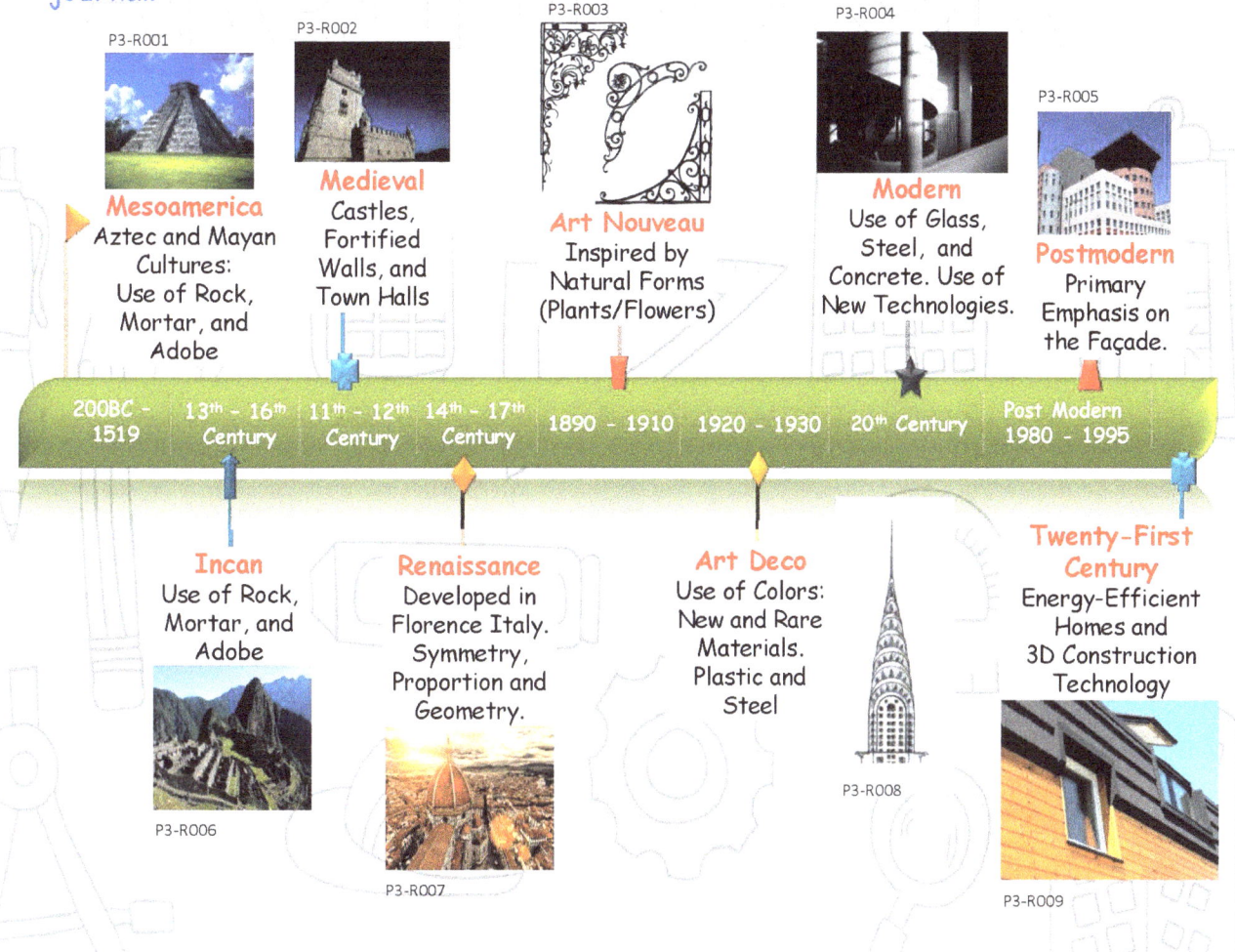

Mesoamerica (200BC - 1519)
Aztec and Mayan Cultures: Use of Rock, Mortar, and Adobe

Medieval (13th - 16th Century)
Castles, Fortified Walls, and Town Halls

Art Nouveau (1890 - 1910)
Inspired by Natural Forms (Plants/Flowers)

Modern (20th Century)
Use of Glass, Steel, and Concrete. Use of New Technologies.

Postmodern (Post Modern 1980 - 1995)
Primary Emphasis on the Façade.

Incan (11th - 12th Century)
Use of Rock, Mortar, and Adobe

Renaissance (14th - 17th Century)
Developed in Florence Italy. Symmetry, Proportion and Geometry.

Art Deco (1920 - 1930)
Use of Colors: New and Rare Materials. Plastic and Steel

Twenty-First Century
Energy-Efficient Homes and 3D Construction Technology

Do some research and see how design has evolved throughout history. Each culture has different needs and ways to see and perceive things. The different architecture styles are influenced by cultural diversity.

Photo Credits are located in the Index Page.

3

The following is a selected list of famous architects and their legacies. When I was a student the vision and design concepts of these architects, and others immediately influenced me. Do some research and see what other information you can find about them.

Antoni Gaudi
1852-1926
Spanish architect

Period: Art nouveau
Legacy: Casa Batllo

Casa Batllo is a masterpiece. The façade shows marine and organic elements, represented by pieces of glass and ceramic. Gaudi avoided straight lines in the entire building. It is a combination of design, color, irregular shapes, and light.

Filippo Brunelleschi
1377-1446
Italian architect

Period: Renaissance
Legacy: Dome of Santa Maria del Fiore

The dome of Santa Maria del Fiore is the most important architectural effort of the Renaissance. Brunelleschi used a new dome design with no supports, based on a brick pattern normally used on floors.

William Van Alen
1883-1954
American architect

Period: Art deco
Legacy: Chrysler Building

The Chrysler Building is supported by a steel skeleton, concrete, and stainless steel on the exterior. The building was finished on May 27, 1930, and is 319 meters (1,047 feet) high with seventy-seven floors, including a three-story-high lobby. It was named a New York City landmark in 1978.

Photo Credits are located in the Index Page.

Frank Lloyd Wright
1867-1959
American architect

Period: Modern
Legacy: Solomon R. Guggenheim Museum

P5-R001

The Guggenheim Museum opened its doors on October 21, 1959. It took Wright sixteen years to complete the design and he died before the completion of the project. The cylindrical design is wider at the top and the interior ramps were intended to provide a natural flow.

P5-R002

Dame Zaha Mohammad Hadid
1950 - 2016
British - Iraqi architect

Period: Twenty-first century
Legacy: Guangzhou Opera House

The Guangzhou Opera House is a mixture of glass and granite. The design was inspired on rock pebbles from the Pearl River (next to the project). The project used seventy-five thousand stone panels on the exterior and fiberglass and resin on the interior.

Photo Credits are located in the Index Page.

Famous Architects and Their Legacies

Architecture for Kids

First Steps of Design

Photo Credit: moodboard/Collection: moodboard/Thinkstock 82632218

Creativity + Imagination + Ideas

The Architect's Tools:

1. Drawing Tools

- Paper or sketchbook
- Drafting pencils
- Pens and markers
- Erasers

2. Measuring Tools

- Triangular scales
- Compasses
- Parallel gliders
- Rulers

3. Cutting Tools for Models

- Cutting mat
- Specialized cut blades

4. Computer Software (CAD)

- Computer design technology allows architects to create and present their designs in two or three dimensions.

Photo Credit: Rogotanie/Collection: iStock/Thinkstock 490433488

First Steps of Design

Each concept or design starts with an **idea** or a client request.

Then, architects move to the design definition. What are the needs of the project?

If for example, we want to design a house, we need to ask some questions. How many bedrooms do we need? Bathrooms? Kitchen? Living Room? Dining Room? Study?

How the areas are going to be connected? (private and public areas).

The relationship between the areas is key in a good project. Do you want your bedroom next to the kitchen?

Bedroom — Bathroom — Living Room — Kitchen — FAMILY

Private and Public Areas?
A private area in a house for example is your room or the room of your parents. A public area is your living room, kitchen or backyard. Places that you share with your visits or other family members.

First Steps of Design

Photo Credits are located in the Index Page.

Drawings Scale:

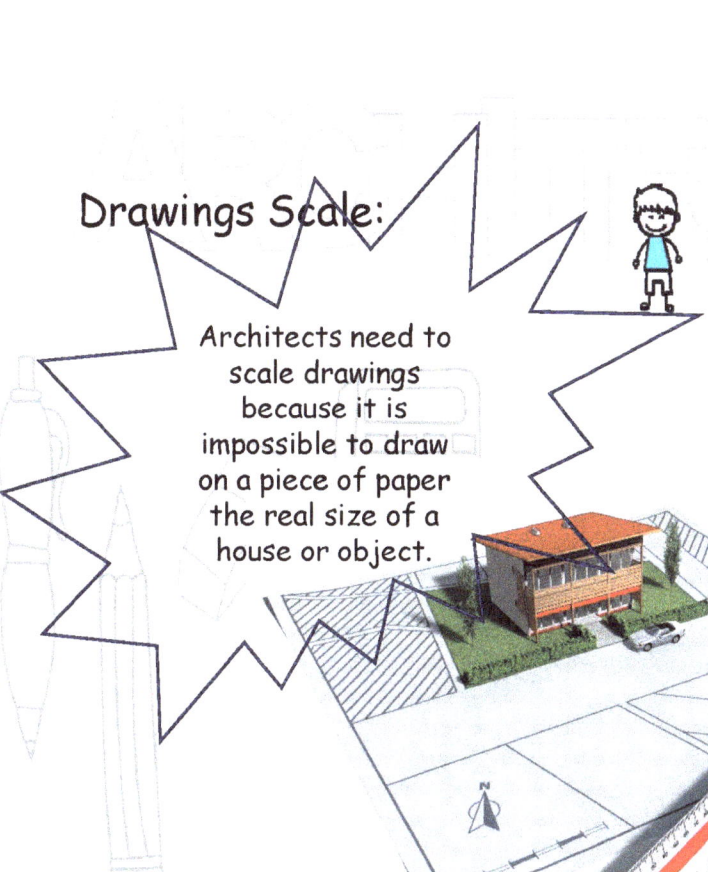

Architects need to scale drawings because it is impossible to draw on a piece of paper the real size of a house or object.

US Units
In the United States, length is represented as 1:XX. This means that 1 inch in the drawing represents XX inches or feet in real life. For example 1:20.

Triangular Scale

Photo Credit: Dieter Spannknebel-Collection-Photodisc-Thinkstock 200317891-001

Metric Units
In metric units, the scale is represented in centimeters and meters.

1 centimeter = 5 meters   1:5
1 centimeter = 10 meters   1:10

The first number is the length/dimension in the paper.

♦

1 : 5

♦

The second number represents the real/actual dimension.

First Steps of Design

9

To the Drawing Board

The Floor Plan

The first drawing that is produced is the floor plan. The floor plan is a view from above that shows the relationship and space between different areas.

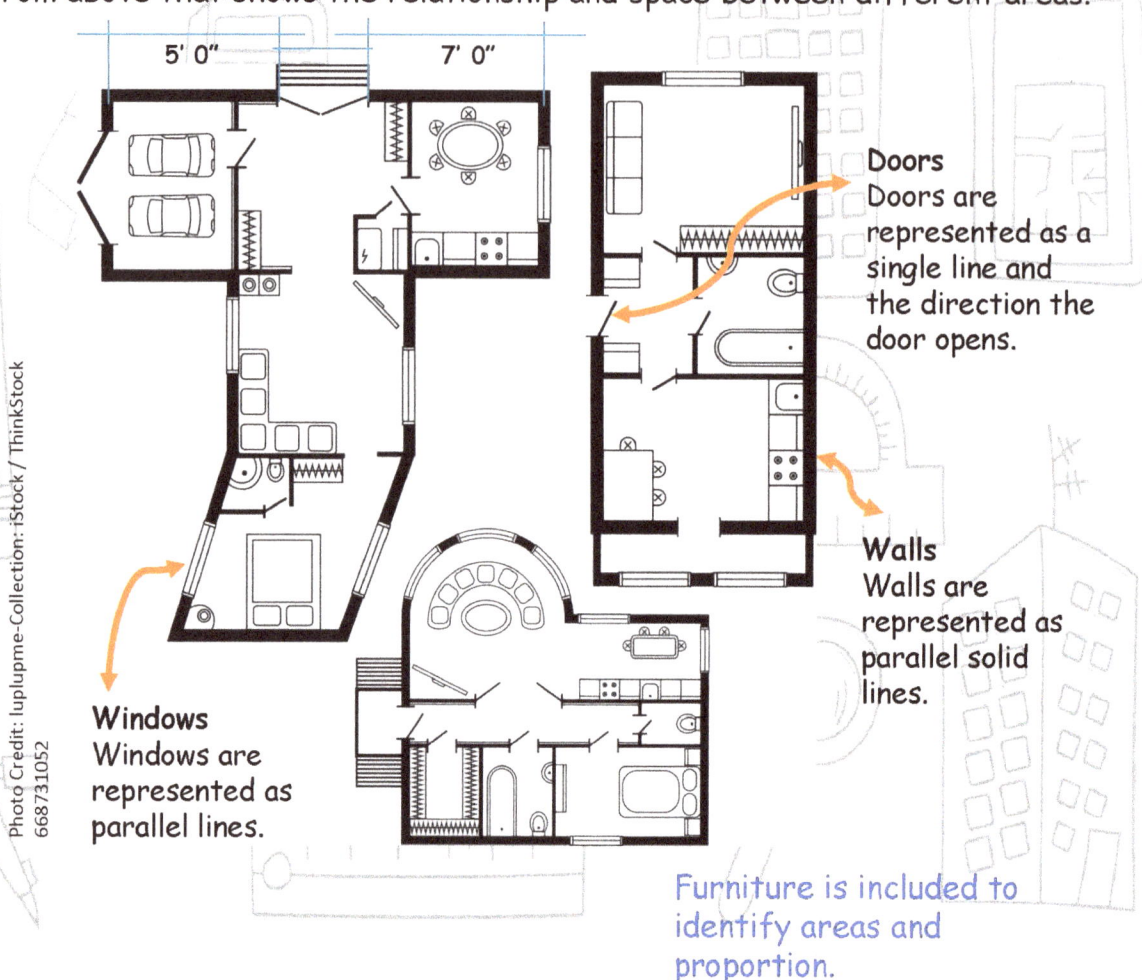

5' 0"   7' 0"

Doors
Doors are represented as a single line and the direction the door opens.

Walls
Walls are represented as parallel solid lines.

Windows
Windows are represented as parallel lines.

Photo Credit: luplupme-Collection: iStock / ThinkStock
668731052

Furniture is included to identify areas and proportion.

10

To the Drawing Board

Elevation and Cross Section

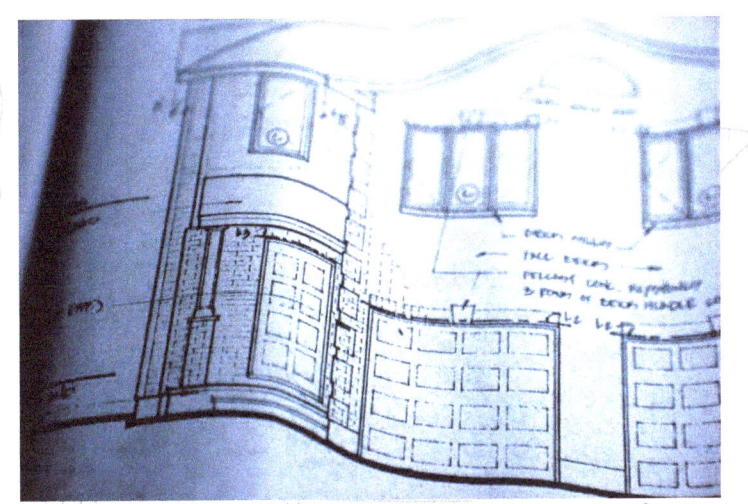

P11-R001

Elevation
The elevation is a view of a building or object from the front, back, left and right sides. It is used to represent the height of the building as well as details on the outside and other objects that interact with the building.

Cross Section
Cross sections are used to show areas that are hidden or not shown in other drawings. Architects show the orientation of the cross section on the floor plan labeled as X or Y views.

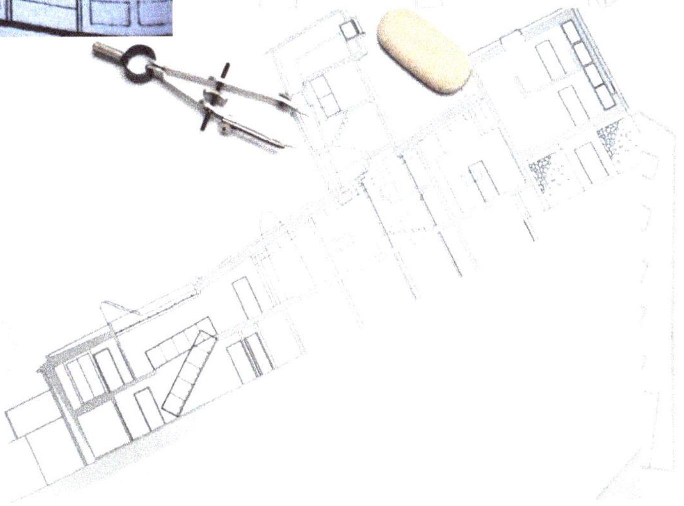

P11-R002

Photo Credits are located in the Index Page.

11

To the Drawing Board

Isometrics and Models

P12-R001

Isometrics
Isometrics are used to represent objects or buildings in 3D.

Models
Once the drawings are finished. The architect builds a physical representation of a structure or project. It is used to study the project from a small-scale real perspective or to show the project idea to others.

P12-R002

Photo Credits are located in the Index Page.

The Forms

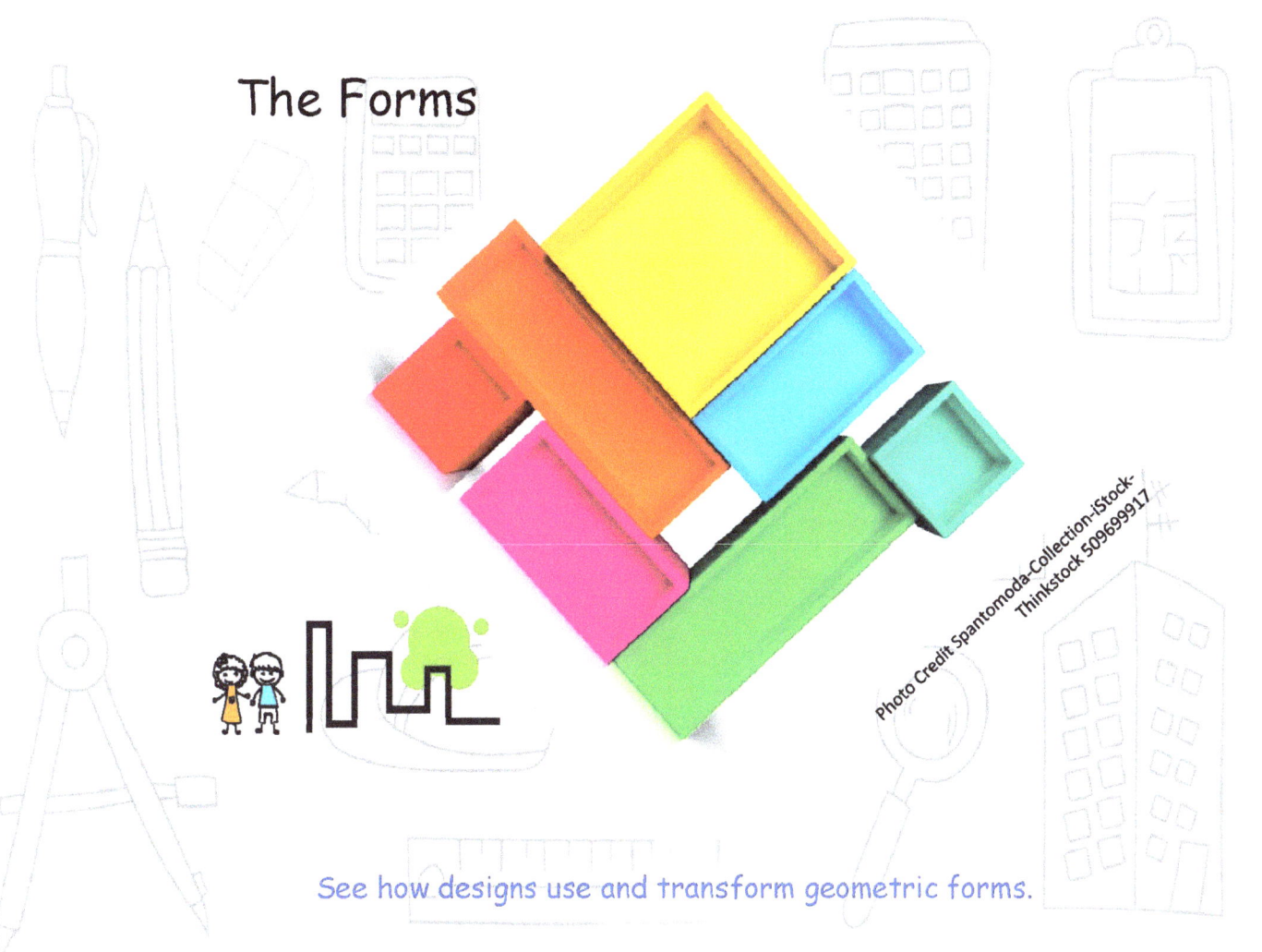

Photo Credit Spantomoda-Collection-iStock-Thinkstock 509699917

See how designs use and transform geometric forms.

The Forms
Used in Architecture + Design

P14-R001

Rectangle

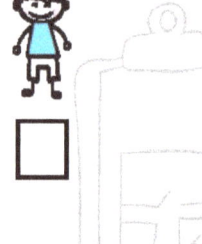

Square

Identify the forms in the building.

Circle

P14-R002

Triangle

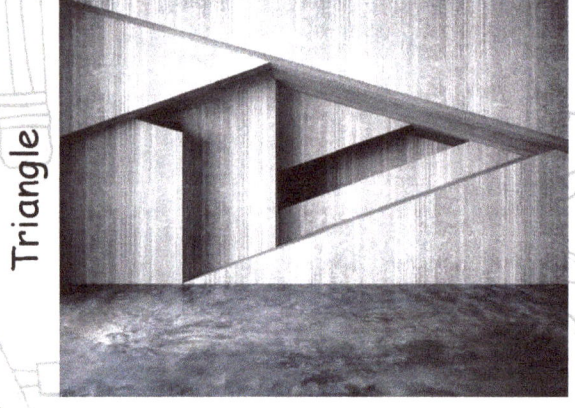

See how triangles were used in a wall design.

Photo Credits are located in the Index Page.

P14-R003

See how circles were applied on the floor, planters, and sculpture.

14

The Forms
Used in Architecture + Design

Square

Circle

Rectangle

Triangle

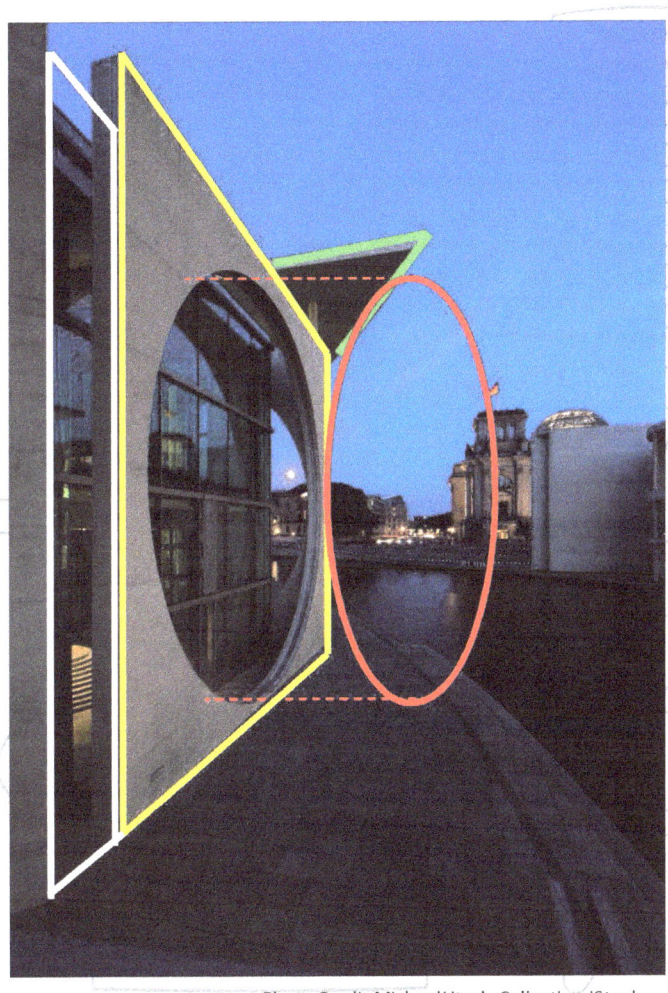

Geometric forms were incorporated in the design and identity of the building. See the forms on the façade, windows, floors, and walls.

Photo Credit MichaelUtech-Collection-iStock-Thinkstock 94398976

15

Architecture for Kids

The Colors

Photo Credit: Ingram Publishing-Collection-NA-Thinkstock 122576150

Colors Thinking

The Colors Used in Architecture and Design

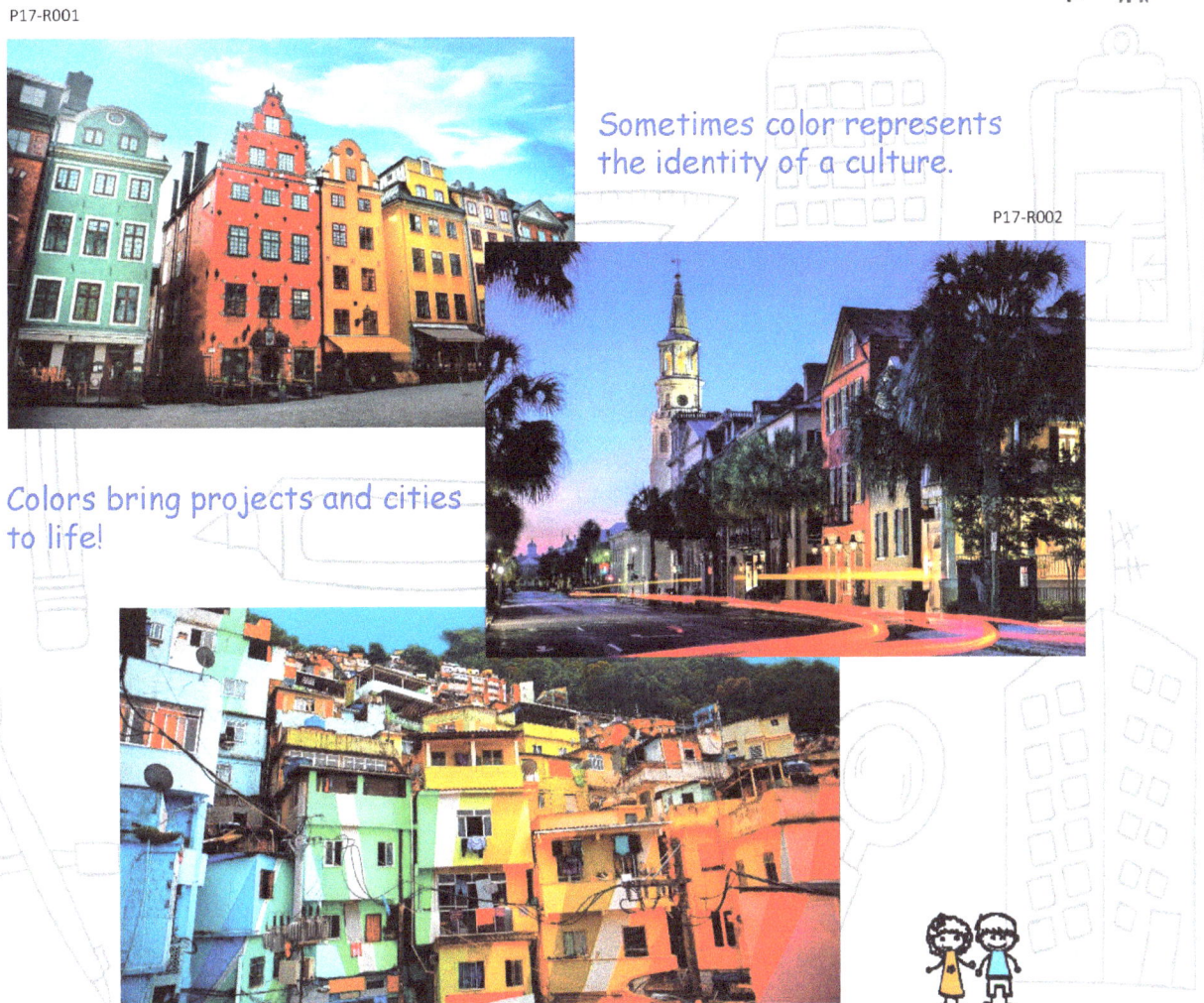

P17-R001

Sometimes color represents the identity of a culture.

P17-R002

Colors bring projects and cities to life!

P17-R003

Photo Credits are located in the Index Page.

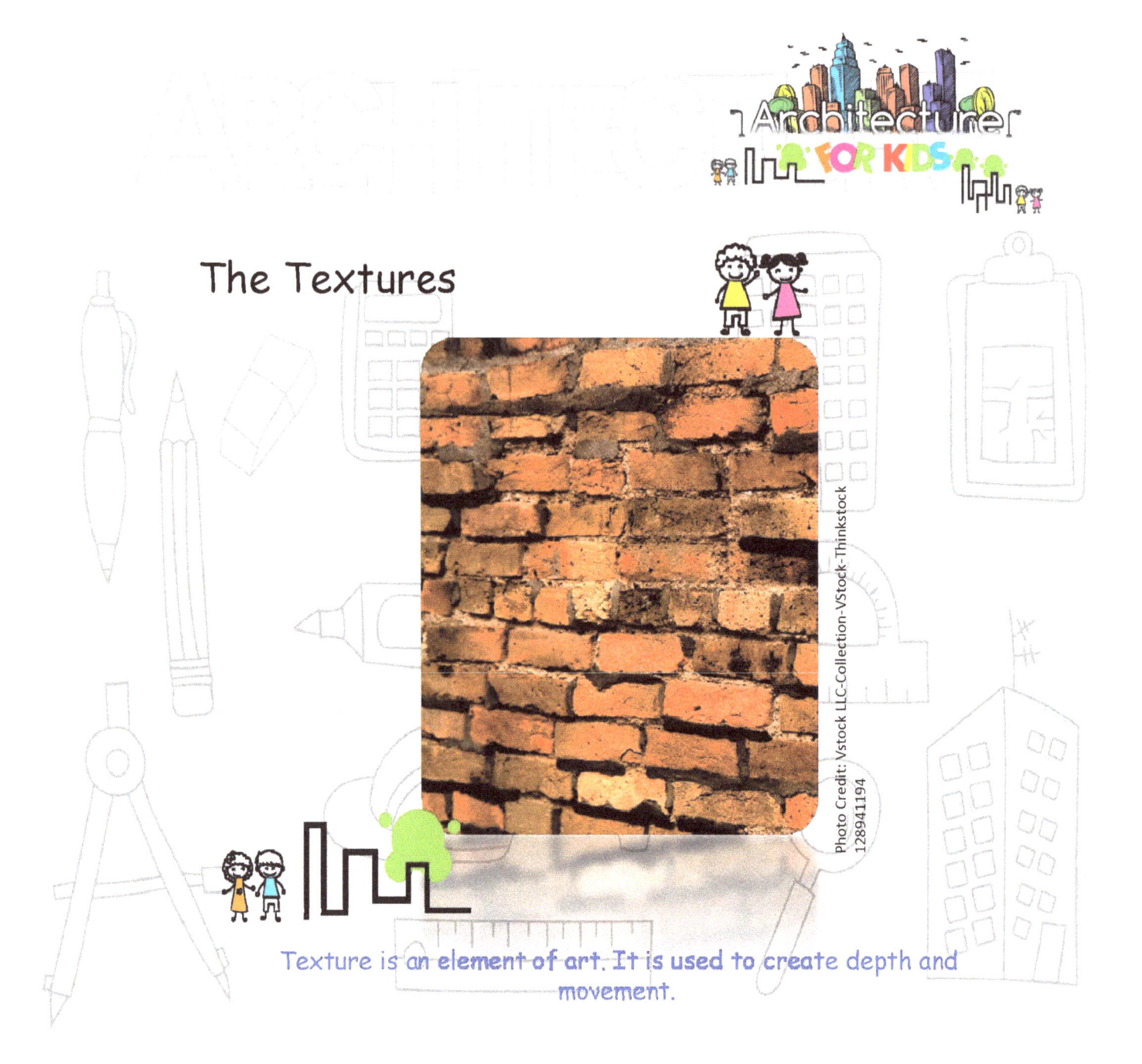

Architecture for Kids

The Textures

Photo Credit: Vstock LLC-Collection-VStock-Thinkstock
128941194

Texture is an element of art. It is used to create depth and movement.

The Textures Used in Architecture and Design

Texture is used in architecture as a tool to create patterns or specific designs. It is also used to emphasize the characteristics of a material, or object.

Texture creates interactive experiences. There is no rule on how to use textures; but it is an element that can increase the beauty of a design.

Photo Credits are located in the Index Page.

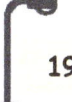

Dimensions and Light Concepts

Photo Credit: Pinkypills-Collection-iStock-Thinkstock
481953684

Dimensions and Light are two core elements in architecture

Dimension Concepts
Used in Architecture and Design

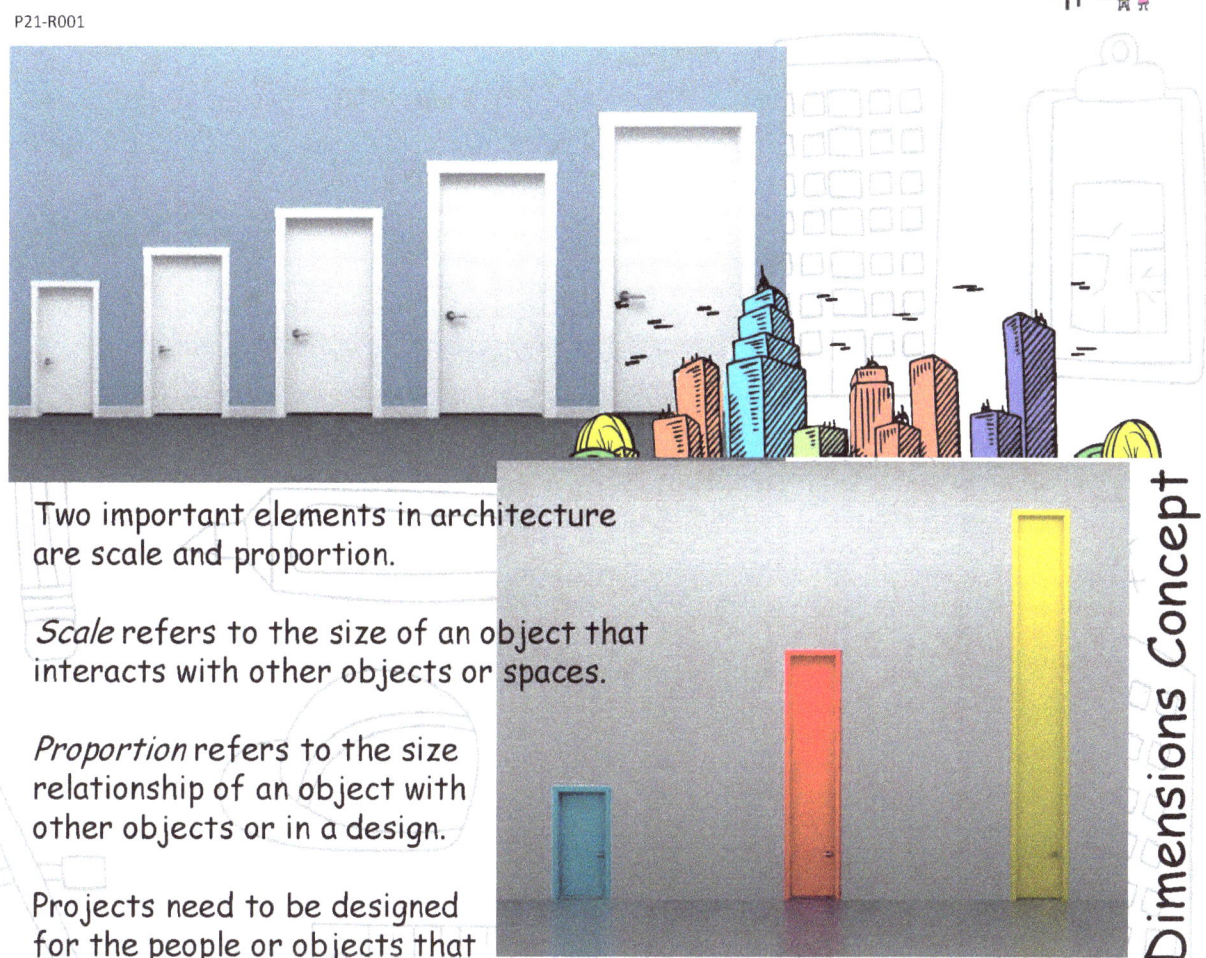

Two important elements in architecture are scale and proportion.

Scale refers to the size of an object that interacts with other objects or spaces.

Proportion refers to the size relationship of an object with other objects or in a design.

Projects need to be designed for the people or objects that will use them.

Dimensions Concept

Light Concepts
Used in Architecture and Design

Light plays a big role in architecture. Natural or artificial light, or the combination of both is used to create different conditions. Light can enlarge or minimize our perception of a space in an area. Light influences the people that use a building or visit a building. Light defines zones and boundaries. It creates contrasts or emphasizes objects or surfaces.

Light Concepts

Photo Credits are located in the Index Page.

Your First Project

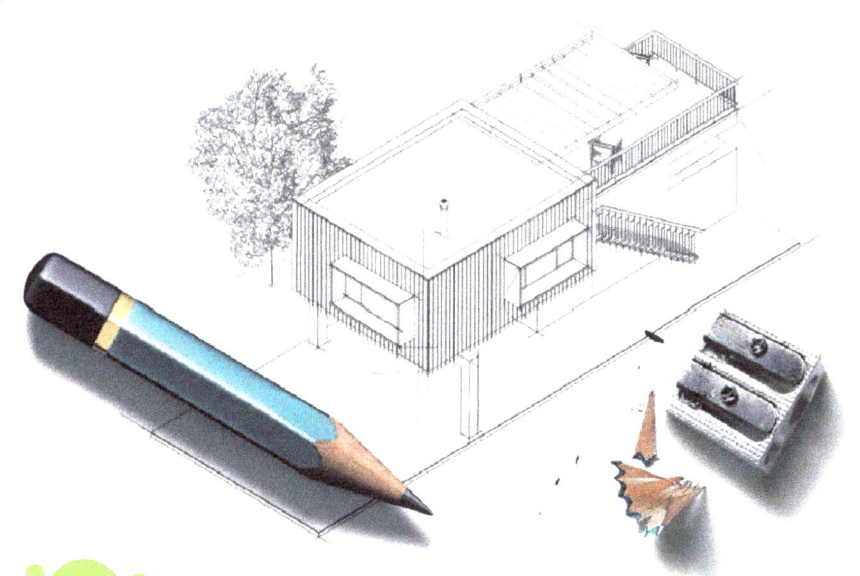

Photo Credit: Dieter Spannknebel/Collection: Photodisc/Thinkstock 200317889-001

Are you ready for your first project?

23

Are you ready for your first project?

P24-R001

P24-R002

P24-R003

1. In a drawing or sketch pad write your first idea or concept. Use your imagination and creativity. Do some research on the Internet; research is a practice that is going to help you in all your student and professional life.

2. Take measures of your room and furniture. Create a measurement log. This is going to help you to understand scale and proportion.

Photo Credits are located in the Index Page.

Your first project?

P25-R001

P25-R002

3. Start with a simple project like a house. Draw the floor plan and Elevations. Do some research on how to draw an isometric projection.

4. Add color and landscape, elements such as trees, cars, and people.

5. Add texture and light.

6. Revise the dimensions, scale and proportion

Remember to use geometric forms!

Ready?

7. Create a model

P25-R003

Photo Credits are located in the Index Page.

Index

Architecture for Kids

Photo Credits:

- Background Image/Watermark in all Pages: *49 – MilanaAdams*/Collection: iStock/Thinkstock 668631062

Table of Contents
- R001: *Illustration of the colosseum in brown and white* - doomko/Collection: iStock/Thinkstock 468111742
- R002: *Tree Growing From Drawing* - moodboard/Collection: moodboard/Thinkstock 82632218
- R003: *Shelves* - Spantomoda/Collection: iStock/Thinkstock 509699917
- R004: *Large assortment of multi-colored pencil crayons* - Ingram Publishing/Collection: NA/Thinkstock 122576150
- R005: *Weathered brick wall pattern* - Vstock LLC/Collection: Vstock/Thinkstock 128941194
- R006: *Man stands in the light of opening* – eugenesergeev/Collection: iStock/Thinkstock 180233152
- R007: *Pencil sharpener, pencil and shaving on plans for house (Digital)* – Dieter Spannknebel/Collection: Photodisc/Thinkstock 200317889-001

Page 1
- *Illustration of the colosseum in brown and white* - doomko/Collection: iStock/Thinkstock 468111742

Page 2
- P2-R001: *Stonehenge flat icon* – JuliarStudio/Collection: iStock/Thinkstock 498531728
- P2-R002: *Pyramids in a desert, Giza Pyramids, Giza, Egypt* - Purestock/Collection: NA/Thinkstock 72969481
- P2-R003: *Illustration of the colosseum in brown and white* - doomko/Collection: iStock/Thinkstock 468111742
- P2-R004: *Nasir Ol Molk Mosque - The Pink Mosque in Shiraz* - NickyNu13/Collection: iStock/Thinkstock 639169622
- P2-R005: *Restored ziggurat in ancient Ur, Sumerian temple, Iraq* – HomoCosmicos/Collection: iStock/Thinkstock 612851720
- P2-R006: *Parthenon on the Acropolis, Athens, Greece* – frentusha/Collection: iStock/Thinkstock 472719156
- P2-R007: *Tlos antique city* – drmakkoy/Collection: iStock/Thinkstock 668799348
- P2-R008: *Dome of The Rock - Jerusalem – Israel* - thierry64/Collection: iStock/Thinkstock 658587626
- P2-R009: *Beautiful sunset at the Great Wall of China* – zhaojiankang/Collection: iStock/Thinkstock 606208234
- P2-R010: *Chinese traditional pavilions* - yangzai/Collection: iStock/Thinkstock 487310080

Page 3
- P3-R001: *El Castillo Chichen Itza (Mayan) Mexico* – Purestock/Collection: NA/Thinkstock 71263346
- P3-R002: *Low angle view of a tower, Belem Tower, Lisbon, Portugal* – Purestock/Collection: NA/Thinkstock 72968823
- P3-R003: *Architectural decorations* – asmakar/Collection: iStock/Thinkstock 470164704
- P3-R004: *The interior space of Villa Savoye* - DidUZeE13/Collection: iStock/Thinkstock 658033434
- P3-R005: *Denver Public Library* – SWKrullImaging/Collection: iStock/Thinkstock 92234934
- P3-R006: *Peru Machu Picchu* - Top Photo Corporation/Collection: Top Photo Group/Thinkstock 126500166
- P3-R007: *Florence view. Basilica di Santa Maria del Fiore. Italy* – scaliger/Collection: iStock/Thinkstock 514232924
- P3-R008: *Illustration of Art Deco vertex of New York's Chrysler Building* - Dorling Kindersley/Collection: NA/Thinkstock 97976110
- P3-R009: *Modern Roofing Construction with Skylights, Attic, Dormers and Roof Windows* - Lex20/Collection: iStock/Thinkstock 523769274

Index

Photo Credits:

Page 4
- P4-R001: *Casa Batllo, Barcelona on a Sunny Spring Day* – MasterLu/Collection: iStock/Thinkstock 454931739
- P4-R002: *View Dome of Cathedral and Florence cityscape* – scaliger/Collection: iStock/Thinkstock 514232924
- P4-R003: *View of the Chrysler building New York City skyline* – Onnes/Collection: iStock/Thinkstock 508465394

Page 5
- P5-R001: *Dome of the Guggenheim Museum* – Nachoanton/Collection: iStock/Thinkstock 482358208
- P5-R002: *Guangzhou Opera House* - yangyang1991/Collection: iStock/Thinkstock 502576254

Page 6
- *Tree Growing From Drawing* – moodboard/Collection: moodboard/Thinkstock 82632218

Page 7
- *Architects workplace* – Rogotanie/Collection: iStock/Thinkstock 490433488

Page 8
- P8-R001: *Idea concept with doodle hand drawn light bulb* - tasza_natasha/Collection: iStock/Thinkstock 481576480
- P8-R002: *Set of Four Buildings Types Hand Drawn Cartoon Illustration* - petovarga-Collection-iStock-Thinkstock 629187624

Page 9
- *Ruler and model house (Digital)* - Dieter Spannknebel/Collection: Photodisc/Thinkstock 200317891-001

Page 10
- *Modern office architectural plan interior furniture and construction design drawing project* – luplupme/Collection: iStock/ThinkStock 668731052

Page 11
- P11-R001: *Detail of blueprint for exterior of house* – Jupiterimages/Collection: photos.com/Thinkstock 87784152
- P11-R002: *Construction blueprint* - Sergey Mironov/Collection: Hemera/Thinkstock 95258308

Page 12
- P12-R001: *Abstract wire-frame construction house architecture* – arhiady/Collection: iStock/Thinkstock 536773769
- P12-R002: *Architectural model* – vicnt/Collection: iStock/Thinkstock 149451454

Index

Photo Credits:

Page 13
- *Shelves* – Spantomoda/Collection: iStock/Thinkstock 509699917

Page 14
- P14-R001: *Denver Public Library* – SWKrullImaging/Collection: iStock/Thinkstock 92234934
- P14-R002: *Abstract wall of interior background* – sayhmog/Collection: iStock/Thinkstock 481907027
- P14-R003: *Potsdamer Platz* – Maxlevoyou/Collection: iStock/Thinkstock 95472497

Page 15
- *Berlin Government District At Night* – MichaelUtech/Collection: iStock/Thinkstock 94398976

Page 16
- *Large assortment of multi-colored pencil crayons* – Ingram Publishing/Collection: NA/Thinkstock 122576150

Page 17
- P17-R001: Old town – adisa/Collection: iStock/Thinkstock 497344880
- P17-R002: Charleston Townscape – SeanPavonePhoto/Collection: iStock/Thinkstock 476461380
- P17-R003: Favela – Lindrik/Collection: iStock/Thinkstock 510083766

Page 18
- *Weathered brick wall pattern* – Vstock LLC/Collection: Vstock/Thinkstock 128941194

Page 19
- *Close-up of a brick wall* – MedioimagesPhotodisc/Collection: Photodisc/Thinkstock 56402838

Page 20
- *Blank interior with window and man* – Pinkypills/Collection: iStock/Thinkstock 481953684

Page 21
- P21-R001: Five doors white – denisik11/Collection: iStock/Thinkstock 506181808
- P21-R002: Three high doors 2 – denisik11/Collection: iStock/ThinkStock 508258632

Page 22
- P22-R001: Poster in room – Peshkova/Collection: iStock/Thinkstock 179983438
- P22-R002: DidUZeE13/Collection: iStock/Thinkstock 658033434

Index

Photo Credits:

Page 13
- *Shelves* – Spantomoda/Collection: iStock/Thinkstock 509699917

Page 14
- P14-R001: *Denver Public Library* – SWKrullImaging/Collection: iStock/Thinkstock 92234934
- P14-R002: *Abstract wall of interior background* – sayhmog/Collection: iStock/Thinkstock 481907027
- P14-R003: *Potsdamer Platz* – Maxlevoyou/Collection: iStock/Thinkstock 95472497

Page 15
- *Berlin Government District At Night* – MichaelUtech/Collection: iStock/Thinkstock 94398976

Page 16
- *Large assortment of multi-colored pencil crayons* - Ingram Publishing/Collection: NA/Thinkstock 122576150

Page 17
- P17-R001: *Old town* – adisa/Collection: iStock/Thinkstock 497344880
- P17-R002: *Charleston Townscape* – SeanPavonePhoto/Collection: iStock/Thinkstock 476461380
- P17-R003: *Favela* – Lindrik/Collection: iStock/Thinkstock 510083766

Page 18
- *Weathered brick wall pattern* - Vstock LLC/Collection: Vstock/Thinkstock 128941194

Page 19
- *Close-up of a brick wall* – MedioimagesPhotodisc/Collection: Photodisc/Thinkstock 56402838

Page 20
- *Blank interior with window and man* – Pinkypills/Collection: iStock/Thinkstock 481953684

Page 21
- P21-R001: *Five doors white* - denisik11/Collection: iStock/Thinkstock 506181808
- P21-R002: *Three high doors 2* - denisik11/Collection: iStock/ThinkStock 508258632

Page 22
- P22-R001: *Poster in room* – Peshkova/Collection: iStock/Thinkstock 179983438
- P22-R002: DidUZeE13/Collection: iStock/Thinkstock 658033434

Index

Photo Credits:

Page 23
- Pencil sharpener, pencil and shaving on plans for house (Digital) - Dieter Spannknebel/Collection: Photodisc/Thinkstock 200317889-001

Page 24
- P24-R001: Startup concept – Madedee/Collection: iStock/Thinkstock 638012598
- P24-R002: Vector furniture architect blueprint background Flat Design – nidwlw/Collection: iStock/Thinkstock 473746620
- P24-R003: Messy Office Desk with Ideas and Vision – Rawpixel/Collection: iStock/Thinkstock 496519985

Page 25
- P25-R001: Startup concept – Madedee/Collection: iStock/Thinkstock 638012598
- P25-R002: Messy Office Desk with Ideas and Vision – Rawpixel/Collection: iStock/Thinkstock 496519985
- P25-R003: Start line – BrianAJackson/Collection: iStock/Thinkstock 542310332